The Write It Right Series: Punctuation Principles

Tristi Pinkston

Introduction

Welcome to the Write It Right series! My name is Tristi Pinkston, and I have been a published author since 2002 and a freelance editor since 2003. You can find a list of everything I've written and edited at my website, **www.tristipinkston.com**. Needless to say (but I'm going to say it anyway), I love books.

As a freelance editor, I notice patterns in the things I edit—certain questions that come up regularly and common mistakes made by new authors. There's nothing more boring than flipping through a six-inch-thick tome of future predicate past subjunctive gerund blah blah blah, so that's why I decided to create a line of short, sweet, and to-the-point books that would make learning the basics fun and easy.

All the examples in the books were created by me specifically to showcase the point I'm making, and yes, they are a little cheesy. That's half the fun right there.

I'd like to thank MerriamWebster.com, the countless other Internet resource sites, and all the editors who have been there for me and helped me strengthen my own skills along the way.

I welcome feedback from my readers. If you have any questions or suggestions for future volumes in the Write It Right series, you may contact me at **tristipinkston@gmail.com**. And be sure to learn about all the books in the Write It Right series by visiting **www.thewriteitrightseries.blogspot.com**.

Chapter One:
Getting Started

Ah, punctuation marks—those marvelous jots and squiggles that help everything else make sense. Where would we be without them? I'm sure you've seen the well-used and overly quoted T-shirt or Facebook poster that goes something like this:

Let's eat Grandma!
Let's eat, Grandma!
Punctuation Saves Lives

That's kind of a funny way to look at it because really, how often does punctuation actually save lives, but you get the message: If you don't use proper punctuation, you run the very real risk of confusing your reader as to your meaning. A confused reader isn't an entertained reader, so we should do whatever we can to avoid confusion. We want our readers to enjoy our stories so much that they'll come back again and again.

Some punctuation marks are simple, like the period. Others are complex and come with many rules, like the comma. Remember, I'm not the kind of person who's going to bore you to death with all the proper terms and expect you to recite them during a test at the end of the book—I will give examples so you can see what I'm talking about, because that's how I learn best (and teach best), and by the time we're done, hopefully you'll have a solid handle on the principles we'll be discussing in this volume of the Write It Right series.

A quick disclaimer—this book isn't the *Chicago Manual of Style*, so it won't mention every usage you might ever encounter. Instead, this is a reference book that covers your most commonly asked questions and addresses the issues you are most likely to face. I also offer the disclaimer that I spent a lot of time double-checking my statements throughout this book so as to bring you the most correct information I could—I don't have all this knowledge deeply embedded in my brain and so I do check other references often. I'm telling you this so you know that it's not necessary to remember everything all the time—the trick is knowing where to go to find the information you need. I use merriamwebster.com a great deal, and I also use Google. You can type all your questions into Google and come up with great answers—just be sure that you take the answer from the accredited source, like Purdue University, for instance.

Now let's get started—punctuation isn't the most fun topic to study, but I'll try to make it interesting along the way.

Chapter Two:
The Period

The period is the first punctuation mark we learn as little tots. It's the most common way to end a sentence and helps us make absolute statements. In England, it's called a "full stop" because that's exactly what you should do when you come upon one—come to a full stop and then resume reading at the next sentence. Without periods, our sentences would all run into each other and things would be a mess.

So, to break this down, you use a period when you are ending a sentence that is a statement, not a question. You use a period when you want to end the thought completely and allow the reader to move on to the next thought.

When you use a period, it comes right after the last letter of the last word. See—like that. In addition, as you type, the next word should begin just one space after your period. Like this. When I was first learning how to type—way back when on a blue manual typewriter—the rule was to hit the space bar twice before beginning a new sentence. I've really had to concentrate to learn to use just one space, and to be honest, I still have to do a search for two spaces throughout each of my manuscripts before I submit. Hey, when you learn something when you're ten years old, it's a hard habit to break.

Indirect Questions

If you're asking an indirect question, that would be another good time for a period. For example, "Leslie wondered why her father was late for dinner." This implies a question, but doesn't ask one outright—we don't need a question mark unless it's an outright question. Oh, and just for future reference, the word "wonder" is always a giveaway that you're not asking a question—"wondering" is not "questioning."

Abbreviations

You'll also use a period in an abbreviation, such as "a.m." and "p.m." or "Washington, D.C." If you're asking a question that has an abbreviation in it, use the period and then the question mark, like this: "Did the box arrive at 8 a.m. or 8 p.m.?" It does look a little funky that way, but that's just how it is. However, if the sentence ends with an abbreviation and you want to close it off with a period, resist the urge to use two dots! That last period will do double-duty, not only setting apart the abbreviation, but ending the sentence for you as well.

Acronyms

If you're talking about an acronym like NASA, you don't need to use periods. Other instances, like FBI, don't usually call for periods, but most experts agree that double-checking the online dictionary in cases like that is a very good idea just to be sure. Some style guides suggest that if your acronym consists of two letters, such as the U.S., you need the periods, but you don't need them for longer acronyms.

Periods with Parentheses

If you're adding parenthesis to a sentence as an aside comment, put the period inside the parenthesis if the sentence is complete. For instance:

Tristi enjoys writing books about writing. (It makes her feel smart.)

"It makes her feel smart" is a complete sentence and can stand alone.

On the other hand, if the segment in the

parenthesis isn't a complete sentence, the period goes outside the parenthesis. Example:

Tristi is staying up late to write (one of her favorite things to do).

"One of her favorite things to do" is not a complete sentence and cannot stand on its own. Therefore, the period goes outside the parenthesis.

If you are quoting from a book and need to cite a reference, it should be done as follows: **". . . quoth the raven, Nevermore" (Edgar Allan Poe, "The Raven").** Notice that the period comes *after* the reference and *after* the closing parenthesis. However, if your entire paragraph is nothing but quote, meaning, you didn't say anything yourself in front of it or after it, then you would tuck the period *inside* the closing parenthesis.

Ellipses

Let's talk about ellipses. These are fun little punctuation marks made up of periods. When do we use them, and how should we use them?

We use an ellipsis for a couple of different reasons. First is to indicate when we've only used part of a source in a quote. Notice above, how I used a portion of

"The Raven." The ellipsis there tells us, "There's other stuff that's supposed to go here, but we hacked it off, so this is the part you get to read."

Another way to use an ellipsis is when showing hesitation on the part of a speaker. This is done when writing dialogue. Here's an example:

"I don't know if I should go to the dance with Tom. He's . . . he's just so weird."

The girl in this sentence is struggling to find the right words, and so we insert the ellipsis to indicate that. In the following sentence, her voice trails off, and the ellipsis shows us that.

"If I went to the dance with Tom, I know I'd just die . . ."

Formatting the Ellipsis

Now, what is the correct way to make an ellipsis? There's always a space before you begin. Then, you'll go dot space dot space dot space before you hit another letter. Like so:

"Tom makes me feel . . . icky."

Notice that we put a space after "feel" and another space before "icky."

If you're using the ellipsis to trail off at the end, put your closing quote mark right after the last dot, like this: "And if he tries to kiss me . . ." There's no space between the last dot and the closing quote mark.

When you put all three dots together without spaces between them, that makes typesetting the book harder for your formatter. Do them a favor and be sure to use the spaces. Unless they tell you differently—then do what they say.

Four-Dot Ellipsis?

You might from time to time see a period following an ellipsis. It would look like this: ...." There's no such thing as a four-dot ellipsis. Some say that you should put a period there because it's at the end. Well, here's the thing—the ellipsis means that you trailed off before you got to the end, so you're not really at the end, are ya?

I checked *The Chicago Manual of Style* and learned a few things about the four-dot anomaly. You might see four dots if you are using a quote that comes right after a full sentence. Like this:

"And Jesus answering saith unto them, Have

faith in God. . . . whosoever shall say unto this mountain . . ." (Mark 11:22 – 23).

Look at the line of dots right after the word "God" above. The first dot is actually the period which ends the sentence. Then the three dots tell us that there was a little more scripture there, but I omitted it. The three dots right after "mountain" tell us that there was more scripture there, but I omitted it too for the purposes of this demonstration. Then notice that there's a period after the source. That hearkens back to the chat we had about where to put a period when citing a source.

Ellipses with Other Punctuation

Have you ever noticed an ellipsis followed by a question mark or a comma? I have, and I wasn't quite sure what to make of that. It wasn't how I was taught, and I always believed that once you used the ellipsis, you didn't need anything else. An author/editor friend of mine shared his opposite opinion and I did a little digging, asking a few other trusted sources. It turns out that there's a little bit of a controversy surrounding the question—who knew?

Some people suggest that if you are trailing off

after a question, you should use ". . . ?" Another suggested that you should use a comma if a comma would ordinarily be used. I'm still wrapping my head around this, to be honest. I've spoken with people who have vehemently said "No comma after an ellipsis!" and others who have just as vehemently insisted upon it.

You'll want to check with your publisher and see how they prefer to handle that situation. If you're self-publishing, you can decide for yourself what you'd like to do. As for me, I prefer no comma after an ellipsis and only rarely use a question mark after the ellipsis, depending on the sentence.

Chapter Three:
Question Marks

The question mark is a very simple mark indeed. You use it whenever you are asking a question. "Is it time to eat?" "Can I go outside to play?" There's no deep, dark mystery behind its use—if you're asking a question, you need a question mark.

Rather than going on and on about the correct way to use one, which would be a little silly, I'm going to share with you some "don'ts" when it comes to question marks.

First off, don't capitalize the pronoun after the question mark. For example:

"Is Mary coming to the store?" She asked.

This is wrong. The pronoun "she" would be lowercased.

Secondly, don't use a question mark when a question has not been asked.

She wondered if he would bring her a corsage?

Believe it or not, I have seen this type of structure. Wondering is not asking a question. It is making a statement. I covered this in the section on periods, but it bears repeating.

Third, don't put the question mark after the speech tag.

"Are you coming with us" Mary asked?

This isn't a common mistake new authors make, but I have seen it often enough to know that it deserves a mention here. The question mark comes immediately after the question, and goes inside the quotation marks.

There you have it—a quick peek into the simple world of the question mark. Any questions?

Chapter Four:
Quotation Marks

Quotation marks, also called quotes or quote marks, are also fairly simple. Commas, on the other hand, are not so simple, and that's why I'm saving them for last—but I digress. Quotation marks are used whenever you are writing dialogue. **"Hey, John! I've been trying to call you all day."** We open the dialogue with quote marks and we close it with quote marks. This tells us when someone is speaking and when they are done speaking.

Multiple Paragraphs for the Same Speaker

Ordinarily, each new speaker gets a new paragraph, and if you see a new paragraph, you know it's a new speaker. If you need to change subjects and therefore start a new paragraph while the same person is speaking, you'll do things a little differently. Leave off the closing quote marks at the end of the paragraph, and then start the new paragraph with opening quote marks. Like this:

"Yada yada yada, yada yada yada.

"Yada yada yada . . . (etc.)"

The absence of quote marks at the end of the paragraph tells us, "This person isn't done talking." If you were to use closing quote marks and it was actually still the same person talking, the reader would think we changed speakers. That's the rule, you know—new paragraph, new speaker. Because the reader knows that rule, we need to give them a hint, through the punctuation, that we're making an exception to that rule.

Quotes in Quotes

What if your character wants to quote something while they're speaking? Take a look at this:

"I'm going to be a wealthy man. 'I wouldn't have to work hard.' Isn't that how the song goes?"

Notice that we began and ended his speech with double quotes—which are these " ". Then we used single quotes—' '—to indicate that he was quoting while he spoke. The most common time you'd use single quotes is in an instance like this—quoting while in dialogue.

So, what is an *un*common time when you would want to use single quote marks? According to Chicago, if you're denoting an exact species of plant life, you would want single quote marks. For instance, the 'peace' rose. I did not know that.

Quotation Marks for Sarcasm

You would also find yourself wanting to use quotation marks if you're being a little bit sarcastic. Take a look:

Martha always considered herself to be "cool."

The quotation marks here indicate some sarcasm and give us the idea that we're peeking into Martha's perception of herself rather than reality. Some authors think that they need to use single quote marks in a case like this—that's incorrect. Always start with double quote marks. In fact, have you ever seen anyone make quote marks in the air with only one finger? No, they always use two fingers. Use that as a memory device. I recently learned that these are called "scare" marks or "sneer" marks. Makes sense.

And the Punctuation Goes … Where?

The thing to remember is that punctuation goes inside the marks. It's, **"Jim will be home in an hour,"** not **"Jim will be home in an hour".** If you're ending with a single quote and a double quote, the same holds true: **"When he comes home, he'll be singing 'Climb Every Mountain.'"**

Now, there's an exception here. Look at this:

Do you agree with the song "You're So Vain"?

There's a question being asked here, but the question isn't being asked inside the quote marks. It's being asked *outside* the quote marks—the "Do you agree" part of the sentence—and so the question mark goes *outside* the quotes. A case like this is the only time you'll see punctuation outside of the quote marks— 99.9% of the time, it goes on the inside.

I should make a quick note here and point out that if you are publishing in England, Canada, Australia, or any other country that follows the British grammar rules, you would put the punctuation on the outside of the quote marks. I've written this series specifically for publishing in the United States, however, so the rules are different here.

Chapter Five:
Em Dashes, Semi-Colons, and En Dashes

These are some of my very favorite punctuation marks of all time. The em dash is so versatile, so utilitarian. The semi-colon is shy, elusive, and rarely seen out of captivity. And the en dash—where would numbers be without it? Let's take a look at each.

Em Dashes

The em dash fills a couple of different functions. For example, look at the sentence four lines above. I used the em dash to give us a little pause in the flow of narrative and introduce another thought. It became a transition. Let's look at some other examples.

I'm having a hard time sleeping tonight—probably the weather.

She thought she could talk me into taking the blame—wrong.

Henry called—said he missed me.

Isn't that a handy device? It allows us to hook two

thoughts together, thereby avoiding choppy writing, but it also lets us use fragments effectively.

The em dash is sort of a new and updated semi-colon because they can fulfill the same function, and yet, the em dash can do something the semi-colon can't. I shall demonstrate.

The Semi-Colon

The semi-colon's job is to hook together two complete sentences that directly correlate with each other.

She couldn't leave the house yet; she had to start making dinner.

These are two complete sentences that could stand alone, but because they are directly linked to each other with cause and effect—she can't leave because she has to make dinner—we can hook them together with a semi-colon. Pay attention to those two rules: two complete sentences, interconnected.

How Does the Em Dash Compare to the Semi-Colon?

An em dash, on the other hand, allows us to hook two thoughts together when they aren't both complete sentences. Look at the sentences on the previous page. I purposely used fragments after the em dashes to show how that can be accomplished.

Parenthetical Comments

Em dashes can also be used to insert a parenthetical comment. What is a parenthetical comment? It's like an aside comment—something that isn't really needed, but can enhance the reader's understanding. For instance:

She put on her red nail polish—the one Glenn said made her look hot—and then applied the lipstick to match.

We could take out all the words between the two em dashes and it would still make perfect sense, and that's how you know it's a true parenthetical comment. Oh, and it's called that because you can do the same thing with parentheses, like this:

She put on her red nail polish (the one Glenn said made her look hot) and then applied the lipstick to match.

Formatting the Em Dash

How do you make an em dash? You've got two

ways to go about it. My favorite way is this: Type the first word and then hit the hyphen twice, all without spacing. Then type the second word. When you hit space after the second word, those two hyphens will automatically form an em dash.

Your second option is to hold down the control key and the alt key while hitting the minus key on the number keypad. You can't hit the hyphen in this case—it won't work. (I created that em dash by using the first method suggested.)

En Dashes

Let's take a moment to discuss the en dash. We don't see this little fellow a lot in fiction writing, but we do see him in nonfiction. We use en dashes with numbers. Let's say you are quoting from a book and you took information from pages three through eight. In your source citation, you would say "pages 3 – 8." That en dash indicates that pages four, five, six, and seven were also helpful. If you just used stuff on page three and stuff on page eight, you would say "pages 3, 8."

Formatting the En Dash

How do you create a proper en dash? It's really easy. Hit your first numeral and then space. Then hit the hyphen once and then space, followed by your second numeral. The en dash will form automatically. If you'd like to use the keyboard trick, you'd create the en dash by hitting the control key and the minus sign—again, the one from the number pad and not the hyphen.

Now, I do have to throw in a disclaimer—when I talk about those dashes forming automatically, I mean, that's what will happen if you're using Word or software similar to Word. If you're using something else, it might not work that way, and I suggest doing a quick Internet search to find out how to do it with your software. However, Word is the industry standard, so if you're not using it, you might want to consider getting it so you can send and receive files from your friends and prospective agents and publishers with ease.

Chapter Six:
Colons and Semi-colons

A colon (no digestion jokes, please) is the little gizmo that looks like this : and you'll find that it's quite useful. The colon indicates when you're about to make a list or to use an example. In fact, you've seen me use it in just that way several times throughout this book already. I've said, "For example:" and then proceeded to give you the example.

Making a List, Checking It Twice …

To use a colon with a list, you need a certain structure.

I need to purchase party supplies, such as: balloons, streamers, cake, presents, invitations, and plastic forks.

Notice how it was a long list. We wouldn't use a colon if the list had two things on it—that would look really silly. We also wouldn't do this:

I need to buy: balloons, streamers, cake, presents, invitations, and plastic forks.

I would make that list without the colon. In the first example, "I need to purchase party supplies" is a complete sentence on its own. I then lead into the list with an introduction—"such as." However, in the second example, "I need to buy" is not a complete sentence on its own, so I would not use a colon. I would just say, "I need to buy balloons, streamers ..." etc.

You would also use a colon after the salutation in a business letter. **Dear President Lincoln: I'm writing today . . .**

Capitals with Colons

What about capitalizing after a colon? Yes and no. If you're starting a list, you would not capitalize. However, if you were introducing a long explanation with a long clause or two clauses, you would capitalize the first word following the colon. A short explanation or one word would not be capitalized.

More about the Semi-colon

You know, I've always wondered if the semi-colon feels bad about itself, being only half a colon and all . . . Again, I digress. I spoke a little bit about the semi-colon in the previous chapter. The mission of the semi-colon is to hook together two complete sentences that are directly related. I'll include some more samples here just to help further clarify the point.

Tristi added some more examples; she hoped to clarify the point.

I love to drink ice water; it helps keep me awake when I'm working late at night.

My back is getting tired; I've probably been sitting in the same position too long.

Notice how in each of these sentences, both the first half and the second half are complete by themselves. I could put a period in there instead of the semi-colon and it would be just fine. However, the semi-colon helps us not to be so choppy, and it indicates a direct correlation between the two thoughts. Don't try to hook a fragment sentence onto a complete sentence with a semi-colon, like so:

She was going to be late if she didn't hurry; stupid water heater.

That is not the proper use of a semi-colon because "stupid water heater" isn't a complete sentence. So while the two parts are directly linked (she's late because the broken water heater interrupted her shower), it's incorrect.

Managing Outrageous Lists

The semi-colon also plays another role. What if you have a really outrageous list of items and you need to keep everything organized? Take a look at this:

Jane has lived in Bangor, Maine; Anaheim, California; Payson, Utah; Elko, Nevada; Frankfurt, Kentucky; and Boulder, Colorado.

In this example, because I was stating a town and a state, it would look really funky without the semi-colon to indicate that I was moving on to a different location. If I used commas instead, Elko and Nevada and Frankfurt would look like three separate places instead of a town, a state, and another town.

This also holds true if you're stating a list of names and their occupations. Take a look:

The passengers on the flight consisted of Mary Lou Thomas, president of sales; George Smith, head of accounts; Sam Brown, attorney; Mark Jacobs, paralegal; and Harry Jones, rodeo clown.

Chapter Seven:
Parentheses

We discussed parentheses a little bit in the chapter on em dashes. Parentheses are used when we want to include some information that doesn't necessary fit in the normal flow of the narration or the text—or that you don't necessary *want* to include in the normal flow. I offer these examples:

Tracy borrowed my red dress (the one with the spaghetti straps) for the prom.

Hansel and Gretel (the ones who got lost in the forest) killed the witch and escaped.

Inserting things in parentheses is also becoming more popular as a way to assert the writer's voice, particularly when writing first person. Check this out:

He walked toward me down the hall, smiling that way he does (that totally irritating way that makes me want to deck him), holding his books under one arm.

If your purpose is to add some spice and personality to the sentence, you can also do that with em dashes. We see parentheses more often in nonfiction and em dashes more often in fiction, although it is a stylistic choice and you can decide which way to go. Just be consistent in what you choose to do.

Notice that in the example above, the comma comes after the closing parenthesis. If everything inside the parentheses is a complete sentence, you can put a period, exclamation mark, or question mark inside the parentheses, but if it's a partial sentence, the punctuation goes on the outside.

Chapter Eight:
Apostrophes

Ah, now we're getting into a topic that makes grammar purists want to tear their hair out. The apostrophe is one of the most abused punctuation marks of all time. It's not hard to use, but so few people do it correctly. Let's make sure we discuss this thoroughly so there's no confusion.

Contractions

First off, the apostrophe is used to make contractions. "Do not" becomes "don't" by taking out the second "o" and smooshing it together, and the apostrophe goes in the hole where the "o" used to be. "Are not" becomes "aren't," "did not" becomes "didn't," and so forth. The apostrophe is kind of like a memorial to the letter that was taken out, like a little tombstone in the cemetery.

Possessives

An apostrophe is also used to make something possessive, meaning, showing that it belongs to someone.

Right now, you're reading a book written on Tristi's computer. There are two uses of apostrophes in that sentence—one to show a contraction ("you're") and one to show possession ("Tristi's"). It's my computer, and so it's Tristi's. Ann's key, Toby's brush, Heidi's glasses—in each of these cases, the apostrophe says, "Hey, get your hands off my stuff. It's mine."

Plurals

An apostrophe never, ever, ever makes something plural. If you're driving down the road and you see a sign that says "Kitten's for Sale," try not to shudder or you might crash into a tree. You make a plural by adding an "s." It's "kittens," not "kitten's." You sometimes make a plural by adding "es." Like, "dishes" or "stitches." But never, ever, ever by adding an apostrophe. I honestly can't say that enough.

Plural Possessives

Now, what if more than one person owns something, and we're combining a plural and a possessive? That gets a little tricky, but let's take a look at it.

My name is Tristi Pinkston. The book you are reading is Tristi Pinkston's creation. (By putting an apostrophe and an S on the end of "Pinkston," I'm showing possession.)

My husband and I are the Pinkstons. (By adding the S on the end, we are now plural.)

We'd like you to come to our house for dinner. You are hereby invited to the Pinkstons' house. (By putting an apostrophe after the S, we're showing that more than one person owns the house.)

It's not the Pinkston's house because multiple people own it. We must use the S and the apostrophe to make it correct. However, you could go to Tristi Pinkston's house if you were just talking about me and not about my husband.

Its and It's

Let's take a look at the curious case of the words "its" and "it's." This is the only time when the possessive rule doesn't apply. When you see the word "it's," you're not seeing a possessive—you're seeing a contraction of "it is." The possessive of "it is" is actually "its." Let me show you a sentence to demonstrate:

The dog took its bowl to its owner. "Oh, no,"
the owner said. "It's empty. Let's feed you."

In the first sentence, we had two uses of possessive "its." Then we saw "It's empty," which is a contraction of "it is." This is a really easy mistake to make, and it gets made all too frequently. Let's not be in that crowd, okay?

Avoiding Ambiguity

"I got straight A's at school!"

Um … wait. We just learned that we never use an apostrophe to make a plural. Why in the world is there an apostrophe in that sentence?

If we took out the apostrophe, it would look as though we meant "as." This is one of the rare cases in which you may use an apostrophe to show a plural. And it's a good thing I'm explaining this now because I'm about to discuss dropped G's, and I don't want to get in trouble.

Dropped G's

Every so often, you'll want to write a character who drops his G's or has some other kind of unusual dialect. You'll go ahead and take out the G, replacing it with an apostrophe, and then your quotation mark comes after that. Like so:

"I was huntin' and fishin'."

This might look like a single quote mark in the wrong place, but it's not—it's an apostrophe for a dropped G, and so you'd treat that apostrophe just like you would a G in terms of placement and punctuation. The same goes if you're say, "Ahoy, Cap'n." (The pirates in the audience will want to pay close attention to this rule.)

Pay close attention to something else—your apostrophe, when used to indicate a dropped letter, should always point this way '. If you start to type it and it goes this way ', hit it twice and delete the first one.

Chapter Nine:
Exclamation Marks

I totally love exclamation marks! Aren't they so awesome? I think they are the best! I could use them all day long! Hooray for the exclamation mark!

Are you ready to shoot me yet?

Overusing exclamation marks will do that to your readers. The marks create forced enthusiasm, and readers don't like being forced to be enthusiastic over and over again. Think for a minute about a poodle or some other variety of little dog. I call them "yippy dogs." They bark and jump and practically do backflips—some of them actually *do* backflips—everything they can to get your attention. They are exhausting. That's what you should be thinking about when you start to use exclamation marks—are you being like the little yippy dog, trying to get your reader's attention?

A good rule is this: If your character is shouting, use the exclamation mark. If they're not, don't.

Your dialogue itself should show the reader the level of excitement they should be feeling. If the text isn't exciting, rework the text.

And if that's not enough to convince you, I'll just point out that we see the largest number of exclamation marks in children's picture books. So if you don't want to come across as a children's picture book, limit your exclamation mark usage.

One very common mistake new authors make is trying to use an exclamation mark with a question mark, like this: ?! This is called an interrobang and is used when you want to show confusion and shock, but here's the thing—it's best left for text messages and e-mails, not for serious writing. Either use the exclamation point or the question mark, but not both at the same time.

In addition, some authors feel that the more exclamation marks they use, the more excitement they are showing. One exclamation point is sufficient in writing a book. If you'd like to use two or more, again, save them for your texts or e-mails.

Chapter Ten:

Hyphens

I do love a good hyphen. The problem is, they are misused so often.

Modifiers with Hyphens

For our purposes as authors, we mainly use hyphens to hook together two modifiers (adjectives that describe a noun) before a noun. For instance:

She wore blood-red lipstick.

"Blood" tells us what kind of red we're talking about, and so we hook those two words together with a hyphen. The same goes for "baby-soft kisses," "rock-hard bread," "pitch-black night."

Notice that these modifiers come before nouns. If they come after nouns, we wouldn't hyphenate them. So we have **"baby-soft kisses,"** but **"The kisses were baby soft."** Notice that I moved the noun to the front of the sentence and put the modifiers after—that tells me I need to take out the hyphen.

There's an exception to this, though—if the

modifier ends with an "ly," don't use the hyphen. We might think that because the bread is freshly baked, we should say "freshly-baked bread," but that's not the case. It would be **"freshly baked bread"** or **"fresh-baked bread."**

Numbers

We also use hyphens when we spell out numbers.

She was thirty-three when she got married.

A friend recently asked me why we put a hyphen in a number like "thirty-three" but we don't say "one-hundred." I thought for a little bit about how to explain it, and then I hit on this: Thirty + three = thirty-three. Imagine that the plus sign is replaced by a hyphen, and you've got it. Twenty-seven is twenty + seven. Eighty-nine is eighty + nine. You can't say that one hundred is one + hundred because "hundred" isn't a numeral all by itself—it has to have a numeral with it to make a definite number—so you don't hyphenate "one hundred."

Another point about hyphens and numbers. Let's say you have a daughter celebrating a birthday. You would say, "My daughter is turning four years old today." Or you would say, "Today's my four-year-old daughter's birthday." Why is one phrase hyphenated and the other not?

Remember how we talked about hyphenating the modifiers before a noun? In example #2, the numbers form modifiers. "Four-year-old" modifies "daughter." You would also say "Today's my four-year-old's birthday" because "daughter" would be implied.

Do not say, "My daughter is turning four-years-old today." That would just not work.

Hyphens in Times

You don't need to use a hyphen when spelling out a time, such as "seven-thirty." The correct usage would be **"seven thirty."**

Chapter Eleven:
Commas

Commas are the most misused of all punctuation marks.

Why? Because they do so many things and they have so many rules. If you were to say to your average bloke, "How do you use a period correctly?" you'd get a very simple answer. The same goes for a question mark. But if you say, "How do you use a comma correctly?" you'd have to sit through quite a long explanation.

Some feel that the more commas, the better. However, you can't just throw commas in wherever you feel like it. They each serve a purpose. They each add a nuance. They can change the meanings of sentences.

I've heard people say, "Don't you just use a comma wherever you'd pause while you're reading?" Well, yes and no. That's one of many ways to gauge it, but it's not foolproof because there are times when you need a comma when you wouldn't naturally pause, and there are times when you'd pause where there wouldn't be a comma. And I don't think every reader pauses in the same place anyway.

I've also heard people say, "Can't you take out the word 'and' and put a comma in there instead?" Well, again, yes and no. That works in a few instances, certainly, but not in all. In fact, I'd say, not in most. If that's the rule of thumb you use, you're going to end up with a whole lot of comma splices, and that's not what we want.

It's important to understand the basics of comma usage so your meaning comes across the way you intend it. Let's start out really simply.

Hooking On a Fragment Sentence

A comma is used to hook together a sentence and a fragment sentence. Like so: **I'm going to the store today, hoping to get there before it starts to rain.**

Notice that "I'm going to the store today" is a complete sentence. However, "hoping to get there before it starts to rain" is a fragment. I can hook these together with a comma for that very reason. It also helps a lot that the two are related. I wouldn't say: **I'm going to the store today, hoping I can find a match for my black sock in the dryer.** That would just create a massive "Huh?"

Comma Splices

Please take note that I said the comma is good to hook on a *fragment* sentence. You can't hook together two complete sentences with a comma, like so: **Jane and I are going to the store, we decided that we really should buy umbrellas.** By putting that comma between two full sentences, we just made a comma splice, which is a no-no.

You have a couple of choices for how to fix a comma splice. First, you could throw in another word—**because we decided that we really should buy umbrellas**. See how nicely "because" bridges the gap?

You could also make two sentences: **Jane and I are going to the store. We decided that we really should buy umbrellas.**

This would also be a great place to use the semi-colon: **Jane and I are going to the store; we decided that we really should buy umbrellas.**

Just remember—if there are two complete sentences, you can't hook them together with a comma. This is actually the #1 mistake I see as an editor when it comes to commas.

Making Lists

You will want to use commas when making a list. **Sally is going to buy cheese, wine, milk, crackers, thread, and a notebook.** If you didn't have commas separating out those elements, it would be a rather jumbled mess.

Please notice that I put a comma before the last item. In years gone by, it was considered wrong to put a comma between the last two items. It's called the Harvard comma or the Oxford comma.

I will point out one thing—some style guides don't much care for the Oxford comma. You'll want to check with your publisher and see what they prefer, but if you're self-publishing, you will make the decision for yourself. I personally prefer the Oxford comma, and there are times when it's downright necessary.

For instance: **I brought my dogs, purse and lipstick.** This sounds like the dogs are named "Purse" and "Lipstick"—which really aren't bad names, but that's not what was meant. However, if you use that Oxford comma, this line becomes: **I brought my dogs, purse, and lipstick.** Now we can distinguish the real meaning.

Commas in Dialogue

Next, you will use a comma when you are addressing a character in dialogue. For instance: **"Come here, Betty. Let's see what Clyde brought us from Tallahassee."** Notice that the speaker (we'll call him Bud) is talking directly to Betty. There's a comma between her name and the rest of the sentence. Also notice that we're talking *about* Clyde and not *to* him, so we don't need to put commas around his name. He might feel a little sad about that, but he'll have his turn in the limelight soon enough, I'm sure.

You will use a comma when you're hooking a speech tag onto dialogue. **"I'm sure glad you liked your little souvenirs," Clyde said.** (See, I told you he'd get a turn.) Speech tags are phrases such as "he said," "he thought," "she asked," "he replied," etc. These are all attached to the dialogue with a comma. Beats, on the other hand—actions used in place of tags—are always hooked on with periods. **"I'm sure glad you liked your little souvenirs." Clyde grinned, showing off his yellow teeth.**

Dependent Clauses

A dependent clause adds information to the sentence, but it can't stand on its own as a complete thought. Dependent clauses need to be separated from the rest of the sentence with a comma. For instance (the dependent clause is in italics):

As soon as we get paid, **we'll go shoe shopping.**

If George doesn't call, **I'm going to go out with Fred.**

Because it's still raining, **we'll stay inside and watch a movie.**

Notice that the second half of each of these sentences is complete and can stand alone. Those are independent clauses.

Sticking Two Thoughts Together—Conjunctions

Ann ate a hamburger, and Jill teased her for having onion breath.

It's true that we could break this sentence up into two sentences, but sometimes we want a longer sentence made up of separate thoughts. The addition of the comma and "and" there in the middle make this work. You would do the same with other conjunctions, like this (the conjunctions are in italics):

I was hesitant to ask, *yet* was relieved at the answer.

I tried to look graceful, *but* I tripped when I entered the room.

She was excited to see him, *so* she ran down the street when she saw his car.

Some feel that if the sentence is short, you don't need the comma. This is actually a sticking point for some editors and might cause interesting discussions around the dinner table or at writing conventions. Each reference I've checked, though, encourages the use of the comma before a conjunction. Do not, however, use a comma *after* a conjunction. "I was late for work, but, my boss forgave me." This sentence is incorrect. The comma after "but" should not be there.

Exceptions to What I Just Said …

Above, we discussed putting a comma in front of a conjunction. However, there are a couple of times when that isn't an iron-clad rule.

First, think of the expression "oldie but goodie." That's a time when a comma before "but" would be incorrect. And what about "tried and true?" Again, no comma there. Use your good judgment and don't throw in a comma just because there's a conjunction in use—they don't always call for a comma.

Another exception would be when you're varying sentence structure. Look, if you will, at this:

Jane picked a book and Tom chose a candy bar, and together they walked up to the cash register.

If we were real sticklers, we'd put a comma after "Jane picked a book." But in this case, because "Jane picked a book" is such a short clause and "Tom chose a candy bar" is another short clause, it works to leave out that comma and let the comma before "and together" do the job.

When Changing Tense

It's important to use a comma when changing tense. For instance:

Maggie turned and walked over to the closet, wishing she didn't have to wear a sweater.

In this sentence, "turned" and "walked" end with an "ed," which indicates past tense. However, because she wishes while she walks (which is different from whistling while she works), we put "wishing" in present tense. Because we've made this shift from past tense to present tense, we must put a comma in there between "closet" and "wishing."

Transitions from Thought to Action

In the above sentence, we see Maggie performing an action and then we see her thoughts—walking being an action and wishing being a function of thought. In most cases, it's useful to separate thoughts from actions with a comma or a conjunction of some kind. For instance (these examples use conjunctions, in italics):

Cami wondered if John was going to call *as* she stared at the phone.

Jesse thought about his new job opportunity *while* he pedaled his bike down the street.

Here is another example using a comma:

Holding her emotions in check, Ginnie clutched her handbag more tightly against her chest. (This example also uses an introductory phrase there at the beginning, which also calls for a comma—keep reading to learn more about introductory phrases.)

Indicating Opposites

Use a comma when you're showing two opposites or a contrast. For instance:

"She was a talented, yet shy, singer."

Introductory Phrases

Take a look at these sentences:

I'm going to the store. However, I'm not buying very much. That being the case, I'm sure to save some money. Because of this, I'll be able to buy what I really want later.

Each phrase before a comma was an introductory phrase. Those work to alert the reader about a change of thought ("however") or to introduce a reason ("that being the case"). Introductory phrases are always separated from the rest of the sentence with a comma.

Commas with Interjections

Interjections are words like **well, indeed, hey, jeepers, wow,** etc. They're used to express surprise, command, emphasis, or a change of subject. The following sentences demonstrate the need for a comma after an interjection (the interjection is in italics):

***Hey*, why are you leaving so soon?**

I was shocked; *indeed*, I was offended.

Wow, that caught me off guard.

Commas in Dates

So, where do you put a comma in a date?

July 4th, 1776 (Use a comma to separate the month and year.)

July 4th, 1776, is one of the most famous dates in history. (Use a comma to separate the year from the rest of the sentence.)

Thursday, July 4th, 1776, is a date we are asked to remember. (Use a comma to separate the day of the week from the rest of the date.)

However, if you're just saying, "Monday is the big math test," that doesn't require a comma.

Commas in Place Names

When you name a place, it's not necessary to put a comma after the name of a town when that's all you're using.

"Was your flight from Chicago bumpy?"

However, if you're naming the state as well, you not only need a comma to separate the town from the state, but from the rest of the sentence as well.

"I come from Salt Lake City, Utah, and it was a great place to grow up."

You'd also use a comma to separate the county, if you had a reason to name the county—this won't come up often, though.

"When I did my genealogy, I learned that my grandpa came from Provo, Utah County, Utah."

And you would also use a comma to separate the country. **"I spent a summer in Hamburg, Germany."**

Now, a note about towns, states, and countries. Some towns are so famous that it's not necessary to name the state or the country. For instance, you don't need to say "San Francisco, California" because pretty much everyone knows where San Francisco is. The same goes for Tokyo, Sydney, Detroit, Cincinnati, etc. But if you're talking about a smaller place like Nephi, Utah, definitely name the state, at least the first time you mention it. And of course there are several towns by the same name all over the country—take Farmington, for instance. I could mean Farmington, Utah, or Farmington, New Mexico, or any number of other Farmingtons—there are around thirty of them just in the U.S.

Restrictive and Nonrestrictive Clauses

A restrictive clause is a clause inserted in a sentence that we really need for clarity. Like so (the restrictive clause is in italics):

The man *who wore the red tie* won the competition.

The fact that he's wearing a red tie tells you which man won. If we took out that clause, you wouldn't know who to congratulate.

However, what if you know who he is, and the fact that he's wearing a red tie is just icing on the cake?

Herbert Jones, *who wore a red tie*, won the competition.

This now becomes a nonrestrictive clause because it's not needed. And because it's nonrestrictive, we put commas on either side of it. You could take out the stuff between the commas and still know who won, so the fact that he's wearing a red tie is just an extra detail.

Commas with "Too"

This seems to be a concept that confuses many authors—and I'm one of them. Some feel that you can use the comma—or not—depending on your mood.

However, the comma does give the sentence a different meaning than it would have if the comma were not there.

Harry entered the room. "I'm going to the library."

Susie piped up. "I want to come too!"

In this case, using "too" without a comma in front of it, Susie means that she wants to go with Harry.

Harry entered the room. "I'm going to the library, the drugstore, and the post office, too."

In this use, the comma before "too" indicates that he's going to three places. We know he's going to the library, but he's also going these other places as well.

Susie could very well chime in and say, "I'm going to the library, the drugstore, and the post office too!" But she's still indicating that she's going with Harry. Note the missing comma.

Let me give a few more sample sentences to solidify the concept.

"Tomorrow, I'm going to sleep in and then go to lunch with my friends—and I'm going to have dessert, too." (I'm going to treat myself with dessert in addition to the other rewards I've just listed.)

"I'm going to have dessert too." (You're having

dessert, so I'll have some with you.)

"I'm a singer and a dancer, too." (I not only sing, but I dance as well.)

"Really? I'm a singer and a dancer too!" (I'm also a singer and dancer, just like you are.)

"Let me get a yard of lace and a yard of ribbon—and I'd better get a package of pins, too." (Don't let me get home without those pins!)

"I'd better get a package of pins too." (Thanks for the reminder! I need some as well.)

Commas Between Modifers

When we talked about hyphens, we discussed putting hyphens between modifiers in uses like "blood-red nail polish." Because "blood" describes the "red" and the "red" describes the nail polish, those can all work together with a hyphen. But sometimes two modifiers don't work together.

Take, for instance, a wrinkled, smelly shirt. The two words "wrinkled" and "smelly" aren't working as a team here—"wrinkled" doesn't describe the "smelly" the way that "blood" described the "red." In this case, we wouldn't use a hyphen—it would not be "a wrinkled-smelly shirt." Because "wrinkled" and "smelly" aren't connected, and yet they are both describing the same thing, we would separate them with a comma.

In Conclusion

I hope this discussion about punctuation was helpful. I mean for it to be a quick reference that you can turn to time and again. Writers who use punctuation correctly will go a long way in their careers, but knowing punctuation isn't just valuable for writers—it's valuable for anyone who communicates through the written word. Interoffice memos, Facebook posts, tweets, signs in a business—all these things should be clear and easy to understand, and punctuation can help make that a reality. Now, go forth and punctuate!

Index
(in order of appearance)

60

Tristi Pinkston is the Silver Quill Award-winning author of *Secret Sisters*, as well as nineteen other novels and self-help books. She has also penned over two thousand articles for the Internet. Her work as a freelance editor allows her to do something she loves—mentor writers on their journey to publication.

She is the mother of four amazing children and the wife of one incredible husband, and loves spending her free time trying recipes no one will eat, scrapbooking, and taking really, really long naps.

She loves hearing from her readers. You can find her:

www.tristipinkston.com

www.tristipinkston.blogspot.com

@TristiPinkston

http://www.facebook.com/pages/Tristi-Pinkston-LDS-Author/93580049670

or e-mail – tristipinkston@gmail.com

.

Made in the USA
Las Vegas, NV
30 April 2021

22271386R00039